CONFLICT EXISTS
ONLY TO INCREASE
CONSCIOUSNESS

C.G.JUNG

WORK ON YOURSELF
& SERVE THE WORLD

Motto of
The Grail Knights

The Acorn Book of EMOTIONAL HEALING

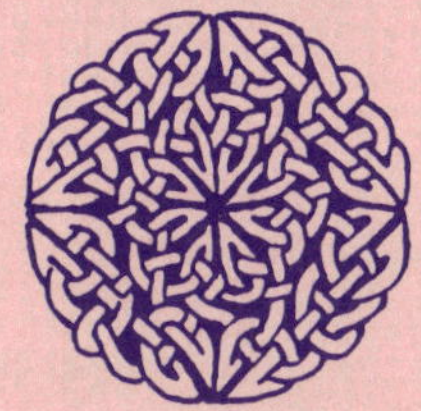

BIRTH of a NEW CONSCIOUSNESS

ISBN 0 948932 06 6

Acorn Publishing

The Acorn Centre
Spindlewood, Watery Lane, Lwr Westholme
Pilton, Shepton Mallet, Somerset, BA4 4EL
United Kingdom Tel: 074 989 338

– Communication and Celebration –

IN 1995 THE NEW RACE OF HUMANS WILL BEGIN TO DESIGN THEIR NEW REALITY OF LIFE ON THIS PLANET AS THEY INTENDED IT TO BE WHEN THEY FIRST CAME FROM THE STARS

THE RAINBOW DREAM PROPHECY

INTRODUCTION

As souls coming into physical bodies, we experience reactions to the plane of matter. These reactions we call 'emotions'. As spirit coming into matter we experience the feelings of shock, confinement, pain, fear, helplessness, anger, violence, lostness, separation, meaninglessness, futility and confusion. These feelings are vibrational, energetic reactions to the Earth plane: the plane of matter. Rather than retreat and 'ascend' back to the remembered oneness of spirit, we can instead, fully awaken ourselves as spirits in matter by working with our emotions: our reactions to matter. These emotions are reactions which are quite natural responses to the confinement of matter, and therefore, rather than be suppressed and ignored, our emotions actually need to be felt, accepted and evolved. Then we can begin to understand and feel good about *ALL* of ourselves. Rather than retreat and ascend back to spirit we can learn to work with the laws of matter through emotional healing. We need to 'land' on Earth, accept all that is here and accept the challenge of the Earth plane and awaken spirit in matter: heaven on Earth.

Motto of the Grail Knights:
'WORK ON YOURSELF AND SERVE THE WORLD'

C.G.Jung:
'CONFLICT EXISTS ONLY TO INCREASE CONSCIOUSNESS'

REAL EMOTIONAL HEALING

To help us get in touch with emotion that has become lost within us, our intuition can guide us to what we need in order to connect to this lost consciousness. This will be something like the compression we received initially because what we need to get in motion is the clench used to surround and isolate deeply suppressed and misunderstood emotions which have been held frozen in lost consciousness for a very long time.

In the past, we have been ready to do almost anything to avoid having to go into deeply misunderstood emotions and we have developed many tricks of belief and thought to keep us out of our suppressed emotions. However, the suppression has become an involuntary clench within our mind and bodies. Physically, certain of our muscles have become numb and are frozen in a hardness that is no longer able to respond along with the rest of the body because, in the past, we have told these parts to surround and isolate what is being suppressed there.

We need to let go of the suppression we have held for so long, in such a way that we really feel and understand what we are doing. When deeply suppressed feelings first begin to move we will not know whether we are still in the original experience or whether we are headed back up and out of it.

We must allow ourselves to bring up and feel whatever experience we have been holding for as long as it takes our consciousness to understand the experience, before the energy can re-integrate into a new level of increased consciousness. When a new level of suppressed feeling is felt, it is very important we do not manipulate our emotions in any way to make them come into alignment before they are ready. We need to allow ourselves to receive new feelings while trying not to use old thinking patterns to rationalise them away.

Along the way to recovering wholeness we are going to find many feelings we did not even think we had. It may seem that the feelings we have about life around us are the only clues we have to the existence of suppressed feelings held within our lost consciousness. We need to go into feelings of distrust. Every time we feel distrust, we need to move into the feelings of confusion and shock that lie beneath the distrust. To heal these suppressed feelings we need to give them what they have been denied for so long: consciousness and acceptance.

We have always suppressed the feeling that God is not there for us in the way God is there for others. We have never felt the acceptance we have wanted for ourselves in creation. We have always felt pushed, pulled, pressured, compressed, overridden, under-appreciated, used, abused, cheated and robbed rather than really free for as long as we can remember. It is now time to make space for these old feelings so they can evolve.

We need to feel the shock and confusion we hold for never being able to live the way we have always wanted to live. We need to feel the deep sadness underneath the shock for the helplessness we have experienced in trying to change our situation. We now need to allow ourselves more emotions of all types than we had previously felt existed or were possible! We need to feel the chaos of emotions held suppressed in lost consciousness. These chaotic emotions have been seen as the problem of creation instead of the saviour they are going to turn out to be.

Without emotional depth we are like robots, going through the motions of being alive without real human response to what actually happens to us. We need to pay attention to the little, murmuring voices within us that normally are not heard.

For now, we may need to treat our emotional healing as a cry for freedom in the midst of an enemy camp of confused beings who do not want us to be successful. We must allow ourselves to feel what we need to feel. Initially, many people will not want to see us make moves for greater freedom and self-alignment. Most people tend to do to others what they have become stuck in doing to themselves: limiting, restricting and suppressing. When we have fully aligned with our deepest feelings, we will be back in contact with our souls and nothing will be able to limit us because we will have regained total consciousness. We will be free.

When we reach our deepest emotions, we may for a while find ourselves unable to move as though everything we have realised so far makes no difference at all. This is a time for us to keep going. It is a time to keep feeling, to keep allowing time and space and consciousness for whatever we are experiencing.

We need to carry on without interference from people who do not understand. Almost anything that is said or done by anyone who has not accepted similar suppressed emotions runs the risk of presenting just another belief system and more confusion that hits our overwhelmed emotional body like another assault. As much as it is believed that the expression of the depth of these emotions is unacceptable, confusion is participating in the creation of situations that make this belief seem to be true.

It is what we have held back and believed for so long that is not allowing our outer reality to open to us in the way we want it to. As we feel the emotions suppressed for so long around the difficulty of the Earth experience, we free ourselves for an understanding and an alignment which will totally transform our lives. We need to make time and space for these emotions as we are able and allow plenty of rest and the cultivation of the love that has been missing in the suppression of misunderstood emotions.

UNDERSTANDING DEEP EMOTIONS

The experience of feeling guilt has been necessary in order to know that what we have been experiencing is not love. As guilt is understood light will be able to expand into places that have not received love before. This process involves considerable upheaval and is not easy for us because we are so weakened, emotionally, physically and spiritually, that we cannot move very fast.

What we need to understand now are the most desperate of emotions that have ever been given acceptance on Earth before. These are the feelings of chaos and hell. Often, in the process of contacting these emotions we are going to feel that we are too exhausted to go on.

The more we have limited the expression of some emotions, the more the capacity to experience and express all of the other emotions is also affected. Where there is suppression there is guilt, because guilt is absence of true vibration. When we have no guilt we will be able to step up the vibration of our physical bodies to the speed of light.

The most deeply denied and strongest emotions which now need understanding are frustration, rage, fear, grief, guilt and shock. Real life is what we seek. Therefore, we must make space and time to feel and understand these emotions. These blocked emotions have been in place since the beginning of creation and will need time, patience and acceptance to allow true healing and integration to occur.

Most of us who are trying to be 'good' do not think we have guilt. However, in reality we have become so full of guilt that we have lost the consciousness with which to notice it. In order for light to become more present, guilt has to move back. In order for guilt to move back, we have to see what guilt is. Guilt is unconsciousness.

Fear, hatred and grief are in the gap that guilt has created by holding back emotion until it has become so compressed and detached from the reality where it split off that it has almost no light left in it and is not living in present time. These deep feelings have become so suppressed and compressed that they feel ready to harm anything that looks like a threat to their survival. The darkness and confusion around deeply suppressed emotions is what has been called evil.

Our suppressed aggression and fear can be channelled by expressing our true feelings as often as possible. Little by little as we listen to our emotions we will be able to bring more consciousness into them. It is a matter of opening the space within ourselves to notice and explore the fear, terror, shock and grief that have been so long denied.

The suppressed rage that gives us the feeling of wanting to strike out needs to connect to its cause which is terror. However, it is not easy to contact this terror until sufficient rage, which covers over the terror, has moved first. When we feel deeply suppressed emotions without being able to understand them we usually become caught in rage, blame, guilt and self-aversion. Pushing, forcing and blaming are reactions from being held back for so long because we have not known how to be and how to express. We are going to have to understand a little at a time and get sufficient consciousness into our suppressed emotions so that we can guide the form of expression these emotions are going to take. Once emotions gain consciousness their expression will be spontaneous and natural.

At the start of creation there was a feeling of unbearable pressure. At that time we did not even know that different parts of us had to connect with each other. This is why there is little consciousness in our deep emotions. We need to notice and explore our deep feelings of unbearable pressure and unbearable oppression. These are ancient experiences that have not yet come into conscious thought and yet they govern all of our lives. Movement and exploration here will bring forth the insights, feelings and understandings needed.

Our survival instinct has been judged against as being of a base and unevolved nature and is therefore not understood. Instead it moves in a state of suppression coming out only when we are so desperate we allow ourselves to lose control. Then we usually make the mistake of acting as though survival is based on attacking what is perceived to be the threat. When we understand and accept all our emotions the survival instinct will return to its original state of balance.

Our consciousness within suppressed emotions is going to wake up from these old patterns. To contact and understand our unconscious we have to go to the place it really is. When we get there we will have the feeling our deep emotions are totally out of control, and they probably are! However, our suppressed emotions can catch up with us with our help. True healing and understanding happen through time.

We have to allow these deep emotions to move as much as possible without causing great harm. We have to explore these feelings in new ways other than in the old pattern that feels that we have to harm that which triggers us. We almost have to allow someone or something to give us the pressure we need in order to cross the gap to the other side of our being where our deep emotions live hidden. The more ready we are, the more we will see our suppressed emotions reflected back to us in outer reality.

What we have to explore here are our real feelings. For instance, we can begin to contact and explore the feeling that full healing is not possible. Begin to notice that suppressed emotions have an effect on EVERYTHING. The suppression of deep emotions has been with us since the very beginning. Basically, this 'lost' part of ourselves has been hidden from our accepted consciousness since the start of the human descent into matter. Therefore, the feeling that it is not possible to really change is the cause of the feelings of entrapment and hopelessness most of us are trying to avoid in our lives.

Suppression can be healed, but only if we really connect with and understand the emotions we need to move. This takes time. True understanding occurs through time. There are so many forms and feelings of lost consciousness that we will feel we cannot understand them all. In time, however, we can understand ALL of ourselves. The most important thing is to become as real as possible with ourselves and others by allowing as much of our true feelings as possible to express each day.

We are not aware that we can understand our deeply suppressed emotions. At first, our unconscious emotions won't seem sane or sensible to us because they are parts of us we hid from long ago. Love and understanding will not dawn on us straight away because most of our consciousness has been hidden away from love and acceptance for a long time. With time, reflection, feeling and acceptance we will be able to give and receive real love once again. ◊

WHEN WE STOP USING OUR WILLS TO PUSH OUR STRONG EMOTIONS INTO UNCONSCIOUSNESS, POWER AND ENERGY WILL BE RELEASED AND CREATIVE ACTION WILL FILL THE SPACE THAT WAS ONCE OCCUPIED BY TIGHTNESS & TENSION

EMERGENCE OF THE INNERMOST MIND

Much of the inner journey consists of bringing the contents of the subconscious, especially the repressed and alienated parts of the surface consciousness, to awareness in order to face and master them.

In order to reach the zone of the superconscious we must transcend the limitations of who we think we are. However, because we have identified ourselves for so long with these limitations it will seem an insurmountable task. By going ahead and attempting what seems beyond our power to achieve, we can reach a point at which the deeper levels of mind will emerge to overcome the limitations of our present state of awareness.

The final battle is the decisive inner confrontation that must eventually take place between the ego and the innermost mind. It follows the resolution of lesser conflicts between opposing impulses of the surface consciousness. In this culminating confrontation, the pure awareness of the innermost mind finally overcomes the delusions of the ego.

Rudra Cakrin, the incarnation of Manjushri, the bodhisattva of wisdom, defeats the barbarian king whose name means either "childish intellect" or "intelligence of doing" - the latter meaning referring to the superficial activity of the surface consciousness. Since we have identified ourselves with our egos, embodied in the evil tyrant, the final battle represents a death-and-rebirth experience that we must undergo on the way to liberation. In order to awaken our real nature, we must die to our illusory image of ourselves.

The innermost mind emerges only when its time has come. We cannot force our liberation. If we try we will only succeed in building up our egos and binding ourselves even more tightly in its grip. All we can do is help the process along in a natural way, understanding that the innermost mind, not ourselves, is really doing it. When the innermost mind finally acts to dispel our illusions, we will see nirvana in the world around us.

We attain the state of inner harmony when the innermost mind finally emerges to take over the surface consciousness. The split between the conscious and unconscious mind vanishes, and with it the conflicts and illusions it spawned. The process of awakening that had been taking place unknown to us in the hidden depths of the superconsciousness now spreads to the surface consciousness. ◊

THE WAY TO SHAMBHALA

THE INNER JOURNEY

A commentary on a Tibetan story which symbolises the way to self-realisation

The journey seems to consist of a series of dismaying setbacks. Just when one thinks one has finally attained a state of permanent tranquility, up surges more inner chaos, often worse than anything previously experienced. This happens because these states bring a clarified awareness that soon reveals even more deeply repressed contents of the subconscious that have to be dealt with next. Thus the apparent setbacks actually represent signs of progress on the inner journey.

The terrifying creatures of the forest symbolise the ferocious contents of the subconscious that Rinpungpa must now confront. Predatory and destructive impulses of repressed rage, greed and envy rise up in the form of killer animals, demons and other eaters of flesh. The slaughter taking place in the forest symbolises the inner carnage wrought by these warring impulses: inner conflicts that sap Rinpungpa's energy and cut off his awareness.

The witches who take the shape of men by day and lions and tigers by night reveal the illusory and changing nature of the subconscious forces that now attempt to tear his consciousness apart. Rather than try to get rid of these forces, which would only repress them and increase their power over him, Rinpungpa welcomes them as his own impulses. No longer enraged at being suppressed, nor hidden where they can fester, they lose their ferocious character and cease to wreak their debilitating vengeance on him. By directing compassion toward the creatures that menace him, the yogi dissipates their rage to kill.

Emerging from the confines of the forest, he comes to the shore of an enormous body of water that seems to have no end. No longer hemmed in by the fear of the savage impulses within himself, Rinpungpa suddenly experiences the vastness of the subconscious and is momentarily overwhelmed by it. How can he possibly traverse the immense regions of the mind that lie ahead? As a consequence of virtuous actions done in the past, the yogi finds a boat and fair wind waiting to speed him across the water. According to a common Buddhist metaphor, the images of a boat and wind symbolise the body and the force of karma. By using the latter two with wisdom and skill, one can cross over the waters of illusion - the vast and deceptive reaches of the subconscious that separate Rinpungpa from the pure awareness of the innermost mind.

The desert crossing that follows symbolises a characteristic stage of all mystic quests: the unbearable sense of spiritual thirst and desolation that comes when one has to abandon inspiring ideas and feelings that have outlived their usefulness and become hindrances to further progress on the inner journey. Here the yogi suffers from the terrible heat of the sun - the searing awareness of his own shortcomings. With the external protection of comforting illusions no longer possible, he must look inward for the means to endure this painful passage. The secret moon he activates by mystically rubbing his tonsils refers to a visualised drop of silver-white semen that embodies the impulse to enlightenment. When Rinpungpa awakens the energy of this impulse, it feels like a cool, soothing liquid flowing through his body and reviving his spirits. A kind of nectar of immortality, it gives him the strength to face his shortcomings and go on toward liberation.

At this point, subconscious forces opposed to the inner journey burst forth in the form of a mountain wind that lashes the yogi's face with sand and bits of leaves and twigs. Rinpungpa now experiences the terrific energy bound up in his own resistance to seeing himself as he is. The savage onslaught of the wind prompts the yogi to make a protective ointment for his face that also clears his vision and brightens his eyes: the confrontation with negative forces of the subconscious leads to the awakening of a deeper and purer awareness. As we have noted before, by stimulating the development of spiritual powers needed to overcome them, such forces can actually play a positive role in the inner journey to Shambhala. Approached the right way, they provide natural opportunities for awakening deeper levels of mind.

We can see this process at work in the next two obstacles. The first, the deadly breath of the giant serpents, represents destructive forces of the subconscious that seem to threaten Rinpungpa's very existence. The knowledge that they can destroy only his illusions about himself, not his real nature, acts as the antidote to these lethal forces. It gives him the courage to confront them and undergo a death-and-rebirth experience that frees him from much of his identification with his ego. In the next obstacle, the mountain of sharp thorns, his loss of illusions leads to the painful recognition of more repressed parts of the surface consciousness. The secret knowledge the yogi uses to protect his feet symbolises a deeper understanding that allows Rinpungpa to face these parts of himself without piercing reactions of disgust and shame.

Having made great efforts to overcome all these obstacles, the yogi comes, at last, to a resting place - the beautiful incense mountain. The sages who meditate there in an atmosphere of sublime sanctity embody elements of the subconscious that come from the deepest and purest levels of the mind. In fact, they symbolise the essence of his true nature, which Rinpungpa does not yet have the awareness to experience directly. At this point he can only catch intimations of it through the sight of the sages. By making prostrations to the sages, Rinpungpa surrenders the whims and desires of his ego and acknowledges the supremacy of the innermost mind. In this way, he gains access to the wisdom and power needed to complete the inner journey.

With the help of the sages, the yogi is able to survive the perils that lie ahead - the awesome storms and deadly attacks of birds and demons. Having let go of his ego and the reassuring sense of identity it gave him, Rinpungpa experiences the terrifying fear of sudden annihilation. At any moment, with the swiftness of an eagle dropping out of the sky, he could cease to be. Vague anxieties that lurk in the depths of the subconscious now appear as demons with red eyes and beings who embody nameless fears. Only the awareness of his real nature, however dim or remote, gives him the sense of inner unity needed to go on without succumbing to terror and disintegrating into madness.

After many days of harrowing travel, the yogi comes out in a heavenly land of fabulous beings. The clear water and sparkling jewels that abound there reflect the pure and gemlike awareness of the deeper levels of mind. Having transcended the fear of losing himself, Rinpungpa discovers a paradise in the depths of the subconscious. Since he no longer clings to the grasping tendencies of his ego, he can enjoy objects of desire without the risk of becoming attached to them: he has found a true wish-fulfilling tree in the deeper levels of his mind. Because of this, the yogi can safely take pleasure with the fabulous maidens - something he could not do with the seductive women of Kashmir. Having achieved the purity of enlightened Dakinis, rather than give rise to attachments, the maidens inspire the impulse to attain enlightenment. Rinpungpa has reached a stage *advanced enough to make full use of the energy contained in sexual desires.*

We can see this quite clearly in what happens when the yogi makes love with the maidens. The sudden heat of an inner fire shoots up through his spine to melt a mystical syllable on the crown of his head and cause nectar to stream down through his body, purifying and transforming it into the diamond body of bliss. We have here a clear reference to the visualisation and effects of an advanced kind of tantric meditation meant to generate psychic heat. Those who practice it visualise just such a fire and syllable, as well as the same kind of nectar flowing down through their bodies. As a physical side effect, they are supposed to produce so much bodily heat that they can go out naked in the snow, at temperatures well below zero, and dry towels that have been soaked in icy water and draped around their shoulders. Some meditation texts even tell the practitioner to visualise the kind of love-making Rinpungpa performs with the fabulous maidens.

Rinpungpa visualises a drop of semen in the form of the mystical syllable on the crown of his head. When the energy of sexual desire causes it to melt and spread through the psychic nervous system, the impulse to enlightenment, which it embraces, fills up the mind and drives out all other distracting aims. Having focused his energy and attention completely on the attainment of liberation, the yogi feels himself physically transformed, endowed with a new and indestructible body capable of reaching shambhala. Only by reaching the level of purity represented by the diamond body of bliss can Rinpungpa enter the zone of the superconscious. Cleansed of all murky defilements, his ego has become a transparent window that gives him a view into and out of the depths of his mind. This brings with it a transformed perception of the world, reflected in the beautiful lands that lie ahead. Everything now appears in the light of its true and divine nature, as if pieces of heaven had fallen to Earth.

The great wall of snow mountains surrounding Shambhala represents an inner barrier thrown up by the deeper levels of mind to keep out the impure contents of the subconscious. Like fierce guardian deities, the peaks take on the wrathful appearance of demons who seem to bar the way and crush all hopes of reaching Shambhala. The sight of them brings out the last of the yogi's fears - the fear that he will not be able to transcend the limitations of his mind. How can he go where not even the eagles can soar? As the story makes perfectly clear, he must see this fear for the illusory obstacle it is. Then, as it vanishes like the mirages of darkness in the glow of a dust-free dawn, the deeper levels of mind will emerge in the form of the noble ones - Bodhisattvas or Dakinis - to carry him over the snow mountains in a mystical flight of transcendence that puts even the birds to shame.

The royal ease with which the yogi rides over the final obstacle in a sedan chair of the Gods shows that Rinpungpa has reached the stage of effortlessness; he can proceed smoothly toward liberation. No longer will he have to struggle against himself. He has gone beyond the conflicts of the subconscious and attained a state of lasting unity with the deeper levels of his mind. Nothing, not even the snakes and wild beasts of the forest ahead, can impede his further progress.

The compassion and friendliness that now radiate from him spontaneously remove the hostility of whatever he might encounter. The way lies clear to the shining cities of Shambhala.

THE FUTURE OF HUMANITY DEPENDS ON THE SPEED AND EXTENT TO WHICH INDIVIDUALS LEARN TO WITHDRAW THEIR SHADOWS FROM OTHERS AND RE-INTEGRATE THEM HONOURABLY WITHIN THEMSELVES

C.G.JUNG

THE INDIVIDUAL WHO WITHDRAWS HIS SHADOW FROM HIS NEIGHBOUR AND FINDS IT IN HIMSELF AND IS RECONCILED TO IT AS TO AN ESTRANGED BROTHER OR SISTER, IS DOING A TASK OF GREAT UNIVERSAL IMPORTANCE

C.G.JUNG

YOU SHALL BIRTH THE ONE HUMANITY

"Yes, it is I, Jesus. I am here now with you as I promised. I am your friend in your life now waiting for you to begin the process of 'one humanity'.

"You seek wholeness. This is the way to find that which you seek. You are not whole because of your fears. Fears are part of God which have forgotten that they are so, for you have withheld them in the darkness of your unconscious. Now is the time, my most dear friend, to become whole.

"I said to you 'Where two or more are gathered, there shall I be also'. I said this to you. I also said 'Greater things you shall do than I'. This means that the greater thing you shall do is to start the one humanity the soul of humanity dreams of. I sowed the seed, you shall birth the one humanity.

"Now listen to your brother for I have a mystery to share. That which you do not share with your brother and sister is that which lessens you, for you are your brother and sister.

"That which you fear is what all humanity fears. Now, imagine if your friend comes to you and says that they are afraid of certain thoughts and certain feelings and you find that they are the same as your secret fears. You are relieved. Now, I say unto you, they are relieved if you say what you fear to them.

"Who will start the process called 'one humanity'? My brother or sister I ask you to open your heart first. The only thing which stands between you and wholeness is what you are afraid of, what you don't say. This is the root of separation.

"I ask you to end separation now by putting your self-esteem and individuality to one side and dare to talk to your friend that which you have hidden within you for such a long time. For such a very long time.

"Do you want to see a mystery? Do you want to see magic, a miracle? I tell you, 'First there was the word and last, there shall be the word'. Fears do not like to be spoken. Fears dissolve when they are brought into the open. Fears do not have power in themselves, they only have the power you give to them by keeping them in special, secret places within the human mind.

"There is only one mind and that is where I meet you and know you, my friend, within the one universal mind of which we are all a part.

"This is the time. I say lay down your ego with love, and, with love you shall find that which you truly are. I said I would prepare a place for you in the Father's house, this is your house my beloved, and I await you. Before you can speak the true word of who you are you must heal each other's hurts.

"You have many misconceptions about the universe, about your Father's house. Speak your doubts, your hurts, your wounds one to another and find the friends, your family, you lost long ago. What you do not say, one to another, is what keeps you apart. Put your rational minds to one side, open to your fellows and you will find me. What you call 'a fear' is, in truth, a misunderstood and lonely part of the mind of God.

"I say to you now 'In the end, when the word of God is spoken, one to another, though they fear what they say, these very words shall be the mystical bridge by which the oversoul of the human being shall come to remember its divinity'.

"I am everywhere within and about you. When you have shared your fears and solved your doubts you will find you are me. We are the same. While you are divided into what you can accept and what you deny you are not whole.

"If you have ears to hear, then hear. If you have eyes to see, then see. If you have mouths to speak, then speak.

"If you have hearts to share, then share them."

Sananda - Your Brother

SPIRITUAL TEACHING SHOULD NOT BE DIRECTING US TO LIFT ABOVE AND DROP OFF THE PHYSICAL AND EMOTIONAL BODIES AND TRY TO RETURN TO ESSENCE IN THE GODHEAD WITHOUT THEM. THIS HAS BEEN A MASSIVE SPIRITUAL MISUNDERSTANDING ON EARTH. THE REALITY IS THAT THIS APPROACH WILL NOT WORK BECAUSE WHAT IS OURS, IS OURS, AND WE CANNOT DROP IT OFF. THE WAY IS TO EVOLVE, AND TO EVOLVE WE MUST ACCEPT IT AND INTEGRATE IT WITHIN US

OUR FEELINGS OF RAGE

Jeanne Segal Ph.D.

Our feelings of rage were pushed into unconsciousness as we learned to hold our breath, clench our teeth and squeeze our bodies to deaden the fierce emotion that surged toward the surface. We had to learn to suppress our rage to conform to society's definition of acceptable behaviour, and suppressing rage made particular sense if our role models were volatile or abusive. We were persuaded, manipulated, cajoled or punished into swallowing our natural feelings, especially rage, for rage frightens and enrages others as well. As a result we become increasingly anaesthetised to the very needs and feelings that triggered our rage in the first place.

Because rage is kindled by the survival force itself, it always will be an integral part of life's experience for each of us. But it is when we continue to deny rage that it festers and grows in our physical and mental consciousness. With the addition of each new denial, each new assault, a last straw eventually drops into our emotional pile and we erupt, often harming ourselves and others. Our furious outbursts come as blasts; tempers snap and we lash out, red-faced and shaking. We smash and throw things. We shout, swear and fight. At other times we boil and seethe just below the surface, our heads pounding, our stomach in knots, our teeth gnashing and our bodies stiffening until, painfully, we confine our furies to our inner world.

Incident after incident magnifies our irritation, yet we are unable or unwilling to reveal our true feelings, withholding them even from ourselves. In time our denial results in a prevailing sense of victimisation. And because the display of emotion is so unacceptable in our culture, we often compound our fury by feeling guilty or by getting angry with ourselves for being angry. The line between sanity and insanity thins. When the dam breaks, the outcome is often frighteningly unexpected and destructive. We have lost control of our control. Is it any wonder we struggle so terribly to put the feelings of rage back in the now tightly sealed musculature of our bodies?

The key to integrating our feelings of rage is to own the raw emotion. We must take responsibility for our anger while remaining non-judgmental of ourselves. Resisting feelings of rage only escalates them. Rage is triggered by a sense of victimisation and helplessness. But when we fully experience the intensity of our anger, we release the energy that will allow us to do something about the situation.

We all have experienced the growing frustrations of a day filled with added irritations. The water heater breaks, you miss an important phone call, you spill mustard on your new pants, your children spend the morning arguing, you wait an hour to see the dentist, and your car refuses to start. You feel like screaming, your chest feels constricted, your jaw is set and you think, 'If one more thing goes wrong, I'm going to explode!' But wait! This is the opportunity to really **FEEL** your anger and acknowledge it. Feeling it in your body and admitting to yourself: "God, I'm angry,' 'I feel angry,' 'So this is what my anger really feels like' - allow you to begin to release it. Rage, like pain, is a guide and teacher.

I would like to stress that experiencing the feelings of rage and anger does not mean we must act them out. In fact, if we fully permit ourselves to experience the feelings as they arise, we ensure that the behaviour that follows our emotional responses will be in proportion to the cause, appropriate to the situation and will support us in our intention to stay open and fully functioning.

Acknowledging deep-seated rage and anger puts us in touch with life-threatening problems, shows us the depth of our denial of physical and emotional feeling and reflects the enormous amount of potential energy we have for positive, constructive action and for creativity and vitality.

Eventually you will come to trust staying open even in the face of emotional storms. Anger and frustration will no longer be so devastatingly frightening. You will not have to wait until the last straw forces you into a confrontation; you will stay current with each new situation; you will make your rage work for you, not against you.

When you stop using your will and emotional strength to push your rage into unconsciousness, power and energy are released. A potential for creative action fills the spaces that were occupied by tightness and tension; and, like any other intense emotion, rage comes to be experienced as an internal guide to well-being.

◊

AN EXERCISE FOR DEEP EMOTIONS:

Recall a recent experience in which you reacted with inappropriate intensity. Perhaps you experienced significant physical and emotional discomfort. Re-create this moment. Touch, taste and smell the situation as well as hear and see it in your mind's eye. Continue breathing fully and deeply and scan your body for the parts that hold the most intense feelings. Direct your full attention into these parts and feel the trapped feelings. Continue breathing deeply and permit yourself to feel frightened, angry, bewildered or sad. Allow these feelings as you inhale and exhale.

Emotions shift and dissolve into other emotions. Feelings move from one area of the body to another until the whole body can be felt as moving energy. Feelings can transform in a moment. Rage can become sadness and sadness can become confusion and pain. Any and all feelings can become fear and shock. Follow your feelings wherever they go. If you go numb allow this numbness to become your focus and soon it will expand into a feeling. Experience this next feeling as energy moving through your body. We need to get out of our rational, defensive minds and into energy and feeling. The intensity that will be evoked during this exercise is the result of tapping into emotions and energies that have been trapped for many years. Be patient, it will take awhile to reconnect with our feeling reality. We are beings of energy. And energy wants to move! ◊

TOTAL AWAKENING

You will be dealing with old patterns, old and hidden pains and hurts which for too long have kept emotional and spiritual energies entrapped within you.

Be aware that your sensitivity to outer happenings will be greatly increased. Your physical, emotional and spiritual feelings and reactions will be amplified many fold. Simply allow this to happen, recognise it, understand it, feel it, pass through it and let it go.

Trust when hurt and sadness come, as at times they do. You are all now deeply working with your unconsciousness and that ultimately means freedom for the whole of humanity.

It is through going deep into the fears, so deep that any armouring on the chakras is cracked and dissolved, that personal and global transformation is, and will take place.

When we go deep enough into pain and fear we reach a place where the All is contained and we join with all the Lighted Ones.

First, the fear and unconsciousness has to be gone into.

◊

The hardest thing is getting our real will to live back. To regain the real will to live we have to go back and keep on going back through all our fears, all the parts of us which have gone to sleep, until we are awake again into the full light of real life on Earth.

◊

◊ LET FEELINGS OUT ◊ UNDERSTANDING FOLLOWS ◊ WILL MAKE RIGHT CHOICE ONCE ALL HAS SURFACED ◊ DEEPEST, DARKEST PART NOW ◊ BEYOND STANDS GATEWAY TO NEW CONSCIOUSNESS ◊ CANNOT UNDERSTAND YET UNDERSTANDING FOLLOWS ONCE FEELINGS HAVE BEEN EXPERIENCED ◊
◊ TIME LAG ◊ TRUST ◊

WHEN WE HAVE CLEARED ENOUGH OF OUR SURFACE CONFUSION WE ARE GOING TO NEED TO RECLAIM THE REST OF US

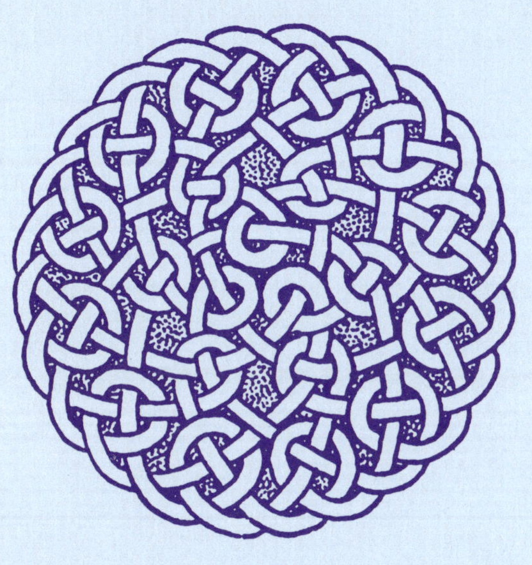

THIS IS THE PART OF US THAT HAS NOT EXPRESSED ITSELF YET IN THIS PRESENT LIFE BECAUSE THIS DENIED PART HAD TO WAIT UNTIL IT COULD BE ACCEPTED BEFORE IT COULD COME FORWARD FOR CLEARANCE

TO FORM ONE HUMANITY

Now is the time to be open and honest about what we really feel inside - our inner world of feelings we do not feel safe sharing with the world - what we really feel - the inner agony and frustration - how we feel powerless to change to what we want - how we feel powerless to be who we really are.

Now is the time to see that we have been where the other is and need only allow compassion not pity, and love not rescuing, to express openly and spontaneously first with understanding to follow later.

To form one humanity we have to open all of ourselves to others otherwise if we keep half of ourselves hidden we cannot get close to each other. We cannot start to have the one humanity we are looking for. If we hide half of ourselves from each other we cannot get close, by definition. We are rebirthing ourselves and the Earth. All the old ways must go.

Share ALL *your inner feelings whatever they are. Don't let your old way of thinking dictate which feelings you share. Share* ALL *your feelings even if you don't understand them and we will start to get close.*

WE ARE THE SAME
WE HAVE THE SAME FEELINGS
WE ARE ALL TOTALLY THE SAME
WE ARE THE SAME
YOUR ANGUISH IS MINE
MY ANGUISH IS YOURS

To uncover the true reality we have to trust and not hide half of what we experience. When we share all and drop our brave faces, our masks, the blocks between us come down - the competition of doing better is dissolved because we are all in the same boat.

Feeling is healing. Express ALL *and your mind will rebirth into something totally new your mind knows little of. Share all now. Dare - risk and see a breakthrough which will amaze you - only a little further - trust - we are the same!*

IN HEALING OUR EMOTIONS, WE MUST ALLOW THEM TO TELL US HOW UPSET THEY HAVE BECOME. THE UNDERSTANDING NEEDED IS, IN HEARING FROM OUR EMOTIONS UNCONDITIONALLY, WE HAVE TAKEN THE STEP OF ACCEPTING THEM, WHEREVER THEY ARE

WE MUST ACCEPT OUR FEELINGS IN ORDER TO EVOLVE THEM. WE CANNOT BEAT FEELINGS INTO THE APPROPRIATE SHAPE. FEELINGS MUST BE ACCEPTED AS THEY ARE AND THEN EVOLVED

EMOTIONAL HEALING

IN HEALING OURSELVES, WE MUST ALLOW OUR SUPPRESSED FEELINGS TO TELL US HOW UPSET THEY HAVE BECOME.

The understanding needed is in hearing from our feelings unconditionally, we have taken the step of accepting them wherever they are. We must accept feelings in order to evolve them. Feelings must be accepted and then evolved.

This is how to evolve ourselves quickly: express everything we feel and do not stop expressing emotionally and otherwise until we have really finished. When we have cleared out, truly, all emotional charge any given situation triggers in us, we will have allowed the release of old emotions that have accumulated when the free expression of feelings was denied.

Controlling rather than expressing our emotions means that we do not have acceptance for the part of us that experiences the Earth. If we do not totally accept our human part first, we cannot expand into anything greater.

ALL FEELINGS CAN EVOLVE

We need to recognise every feeling and thought we would otherwise push away or ignore. ALL feelings, given space and time for experiencing and understanding, can evolve. 'Negativity' can feel good about itself! Fear can evolve into another feeling of greater understanding if it is felt and expressed and not pressured but given time and space. Fear has the ability to expand into love and compassion.

We must experience and communicate with everything that comes from any place within us. We can talk to a suppressed feeling, accept its response to us and find the understandings which will explain to us why we felt we had to deny it. Then we can forgive ourselves for having denied it. Finally, we need to negotiate a new relationship between this part of us and the rest of us and accept the contribution of once suppressed feelings in deciding what we feel like doing.

WE CANNOT GO PAST EMOTIONS AND FIND HEALING

We cannot go past emotions and find healing. For example, if we tell ourselves we should not be angry at someone because part of us says it is not their fault, we cannot move the blaming rage we feel we have been holding back for so long. If we change our behaviour towards them based on some understanding our mind has received, our vibrational field is still vibrating the same.

Because the role of emotions has been so ignored, there are many people who think they can take a 'negative' energy and convert it into a positive energy, when in actuality they are not doing anything but mind games and form changes. The energy, however, is still vibrating the same.

If we are polarised towards our light side, our level of seeming understanding may be our greatest stumbling block to freeing our unconscious if we tell ourselves that what we are feeling is irrational or unjustifiable. If we are polarised towards our unconscious, our guilt may be our biggest stumbling block.

Therefore, no matter how irrational or unjustifiable we may be telling ourselves our feelings are in certain areas, we must allow them to come into consciousness if we want to understand and heal what we have suppressed.

We need to be careful to move and feel suppressed emotions with ourselves first. Then when we have cleared some of the confusion and backlog of emotional charge others will hear us more clearly.

THE FASTEST WAY TO CHANGE

The fastest way to open the space for change is to uncover old beliefs made in error and the pent up emotional energy around them so energy can move. This sounds so simple and yet societal conditioning has taught everyone to talk in generalisations and to control emotions and thus lock up the free flow of human experience. →

Lost energy, lost love, lost anything is the result of denial, of holding it away from us by not accepting it. What was lost returns when we forgive ourselves for denying it and accept it. This does not mean forgiving ourselves for the behaviour. It means accepting the behaviour and forgiving ourselves for not having accepted it before as part of us and part of our living experience. All the gifts of emotional healing will come to us when we really align with accepting them by releasing through expression, feeling and understanding everything that feels we cannot have them.

OLD BELIEFS

Old beliefs cannot dissolve until they are seen for what they are. The inner conflicts that keep wholeness and peace away are misunderstandings that are seeking understanding. True understanding replaces judgments and habitual responses when we give acceptance and allow the expression that gives release to everything of ourselves that we have imprisoned.

MASS NEGATIVE BELIEFS ON EARTH

Some judgments are accepted by so many people on Earth that they have taken on the guise of fact. The understanding that is needed is that these are judgments, not facts. The release of these confusions will let in the light of true understanding which will then allow success in all endeavours.

When judgments are partially released, the energy will start to move and patterns reminiscent of the judgments will appear in our lives. Continued acceptance and understanding of all emotions will bring complete integration and wholeness.

Sometimes a judgment may be hidden in a thought we believe to be reality. Some examples of judgments that are believed to be reality are: everyone has to compromise to get along in the world; if I have things my way I will be selfish; I have to do certain things or no-one will accept me; things must be done a certain way; reality stays the same; struggle is normal; there is no way out of all this; enjoying myself is wrong; and, you cannot have what you want.

BELIEF IN THE FUTILITY OF EMOTIONAL EXPRESSION

All of the movement of feelings we have been doing so far has been necessary to get us to the place of understanding from which we can accept deeply suppressed emotions. However, we cannot move and heal deep emotions while in some part of ourselves we still hold the belief that moving emotions is impossible, futile and hopeless. Understanding is impossible this way because a belief always causes its reflection.

Deeply suppressed emotions are not aware that they are going to heal, but they will heal given time and space. We have to go deep enough into our feelings to change ancient imprints. We have to go so deep into our feelings that what has been thought to be instincts will be changed. This is how humanity will evolve to a higher plane of consciousness.

EVERYTHING WE EXPERIENCE IS VALID

The reason for the need for habit patterns needs to be found and then accepted and understood. In everyday life feelings are meant to guide us so that whatever is appropriate to any particular situation is what we feel like doing and also do.

The undermining of intuition on Earth has been accompanied by another habit. This is the habit of looking outside ourselves for answers. However, when we really listen to ourselves, we can heal ourselves.

Physical plane existence can be as enjoyable as any other plane of existence if we allow this to be our experience. The physical plane experience can evolve to include all possibilities. When harmony and joy accompany the way of evolving, we always do exactly what we should be doing and for no other reason except that is what we feel like doing.

We can reach the state where everything that is experienced is accepted as valid and perfect for the moment in which it occurs. The evolution comes from looking at it for what can be learned.

RECOVERING LOST CONSCIOUSNESS

Healing guilt is the trick that is going to allow the recovery of consciousness that has been lost. Guilt is not consciousness. Guilt is lack of consciousness. We want the kind of internal movement that fills our space with our own vibration.

We are finding that unless we go down and recover our lost consciousness, we are not going to evolve. Unfortunately, we are already greatly lost in asphyxiation and loss of ability to vibrate whether or not each of us has noticed that yet. We are scared to go down into the suppressed emotions we believe we must not feel and we are hiding this fear in belief systems that say the acceptance of deep feelings is not necessary. We are trapped and yet we avoid facing the situation.

The truth is we are unable to move into the light we need to nourish us. We are caught. We can't get nourished. We are really in a state of terror but our terror lies hidden in a state of denial. We can, however, go into suppressed feelings of rage and terror and turn them into love by expanding our definition of what love is until all the feelings we have are included and the feeling in them is one of lovingness.

LOSS OF CONSCIOUSNESS ON EARTH

Resolution must come from inside ourselves where we have made the error judgments that it is impossible to allow old emotions to move and survive them. It is what we have held back and believed for so long that is not allowing our outer reality to open to us in the ways we want it to.

To heal our loss of consciousness on Earth we are going to have to allow ourselves to notice that we have trapped ourselves on Earth. We have trapped ourselves in our own denials and in our own unconsciousness. Therefore, to find true healing we have to release all the judgments we can find in ourselves and let understandings come in their place.

ENTRAPMENT ON EARTH

Each of us has consciousness with which we can be self-aware and a physical body and emotions with which we experience life on Earth and the plane of matter. All of us now wishing to remain on Earth must accept our whole being and discontinue the suppression of the part of us that experiences the Earth. Beneath our suppressed emotions lies hidden the wisdom which will guide us into right living.

The feeling of being trapped on Earth is such an old feeling that many souls have come to accept it as permanent. But it is not. The question of release from this 'trap' is the question of willingness to face the accumulating unconsciousness that has been going on for so long on Earth. The truth is by questioning and then accepting the answer we can discover our own experience in this self-created trap.

The present state of affairs on Earth is the result of confusion and misunderstanding about lost feelings. When we restore our full consciousness we will be free. Open feelings are able to take us anywhere we want to go and have the ability to feed us and keep us warm.

STAY OPEN TO EMOTIONS

Until we break through the pattern of self-judgment and self-criticism, until we feel ourselves staying open to emotions without passing sentence, we will continue to undermine our efforts and defeat all our good intentions toward feeling whole.

When we are talking healing, but not getting down to business, we have fear. We have to feel the fear and let it move somehow. Guilt may be another reason. We may have so much guilt telling us our emotions are unacceptable, dangerous, too intense or whatever our beliefs are against them, that we may need to start by recognising the error beliefs first before we can feel and identify our suppressed emotions.

→

Conditioning is partly from personal karma and partly from just being present in a belief system held so strongly by so many. When we recover our true feelings we will find it much easier to change our reality to suit us than to try to change an outward reflection of suppressed feelings we have not accepted within us.

EVERYTHING HAS TO BE SEEN AND ACCEPTED

Atlanteans saw themselves as focusing only on the 'positive'. They believed that by focusing only on the 'light' aspects of each and everything, darkness would be dispelled. They did not really look at the darkness they were trying to dispel with the light. Atlanteans were holding error beliefs about reality that they were mistaking for reality. If they had been able to see the reflections of their own denials for what they were, then these reflections could have shown them the path to balance. Everything has to be seen and accepted for what it really is to be truly understood. Knowing what something is, is necessary in order to deal with it in the right way.

THE WAY OUT OF THE TRAP

Panic, deep fear and even terror are held undercurrent in most of us. These old feelings are the feelings of being trapped with no way out. When we have contacted and really felt the feelings of having no way out, we will have made an opening to find one. The feeling of being powerless to help ourselves does not allow us to help ourselves.

From time before time we have suppressed our real emotions and so part of our consciousness has had no experience other than a reality of guilt, suffering and darkness. This is the only reality this part of us has ever known and so it is not going to be easy for this part of our consciousness to open to really knowing another reality is possible for it.

At a deep level we feel either God does not exist or God requires us to suppress ourselves into feelings of guilt and darkness. These old feelings need space to evolve. All feelings need space to evolve because ALL feelings can grow into wholeness.

EXPERIENCE FEELINGS AS THEY ARISE

Experiencing feelings of rage and anger does not mean we must act them out. If we fully permit ourselves to experience the feelings as they arise, we ensure that our behaviour will be in proportion to the cause and appropriate to the situation.

ALL FEELINGS CAN GROW INTO WHOLENESS

The secret is making space and acceptance for ALL feelings to find a WHOLENESS.

Having acceptance means allowing ourselves to feel and recognise emotions within our unconscious in order that they may reconnect with us and then they will be able to grow into understanding and wholeness through time. What we really know about ourselves cannot limit us. We can expand beyond it.

This is making the unconscious, conscious. We do not need to be afraid of the process. We can stop withdrawing from the experience of being human and face our past and integrate all the suppression, errors and misconceptions of millions of years of evolution.

The old ways have to dissolve and go and this takes time and generates its own emotions. We have become identified with our limitations, and therefore to expand beyond them feels like danger, chaos, madness and suicide. We need to allow space for these emotions too. Then, through time, we will move on from this phase of upheaval and integration into the birth of a new consciousness.

ALL feelings have the ability to expand into love and wholeness if they are not ignored or hidden away but given time, space, feeling, acceptance and understanding. The opposite of suppression is feeling. The opposite of unconsciousness is consciousness. ◊

WE ARE EXPECTING THE

☆ BIRTH of a NEW CONSCIOUSNESS ☆

LIKE THE DAWN, MERLIN FORETOLD, KING ARTHUR WOULD ARISE TO COME AGAIN FROM HIS MYSTERIOUS RETREAT ON THE ISLAND, OUT FROM THE DARK CAVE WHERE, WOUNDED, HE HAD BEEN LAID.

EVERYTHING HAS TO BE SEEN AND ACCEPTED FOR WHAT IT REALLY IS TO BE TRULY UNDERSTOOD. KNOWING WHAT SOMETHING REALLY IS, IS NECESSARY IN ORDER TO DEAL WITH IT IN THE RIGHT WAY.

WHAT WAS LOST RETURNS WHEN WE FORGIVE OURSELVES FOR DENYING IT AND ACCEPT IT. THIS DOES NOT MEAN FORGIVING OURSELVES FOR THE BEHAVIOUR. IT MEANS ACCEPTING THE BEHAVIOUR AND FORGIVING OURSELVES FOR NOT HAVING ACCEPTED IT BEFORE AS PART OF US AND OUR LIVING EXPERIENCE.

THERE IS NO PAIN, YOU ARE RECEDING
A DISTANT SHIP MOVES ON THE HORIZON
YOU ARE ONLY COMING THROUGH IN WAVES
YOUR LIPS MOVE
BUT I CAN'T HEAR WHAT YOU ARE SAYING
WHEN I WAS A CHILD I HAD A FEVER
NOW I'VE GOT THAT FEELING ONCE AGAIN
I CAN'T EXPLAIN, YOU WOULD NOT UNDERSTAND
THIS IS NOT HOW I AM
I HAVE BECOME COMFORTABLY NUMB

◊

WHEN I WAS A CHILD
I CAUGHT A FLEETING GLIMPSE
OUT OF THE CORNER OF MY EYE
I TURNED TO LOOK BUT IT WAS GONE
I CANNOT PUT MY FINGER ON IT NOW
THE CHILD IS GROWN, THE DREAM IS GONE
I HAVE BECOME COMFORTABLY NUMB
Pink Floyd - The Wall

CAN'T MOVE MY ARMS, CAN'T MOVE MY LEGS
CAN'T SAY NO, CAN'T SAY YES, CAN'T HELP MYSELF
WHAT DO WE DO NOW WE JUST CAN'T MOVE?

HE THOUGHT HE WAS GOING TO DIE, BUT HE DIDN'T
SHE THOUGHT SHE JUST COULDN'T COPE, BUT SHE DID
WE THOUGHT IT WOULD BE SO HARD, BUT IT WASN'T
IT WASN'T EASY THOUGH

CAN'T SAY YES, CAN'T SAY NO
CAN'T BEGIN, CAN'T LET GO

NOW WE JUST CAN'T MOVE
WE THOUGHT IT WAS ALL OVER
BUT IT WASN'T.... IT HADN'T STARTED YET
WE'RE CALLING OUT FOR MIDDLE STREET
WALKING STRAIGHT DOWN THE MIDDLE OF IT
Kate Bush

THE RESOLUTION OF INTERNAL CONFLICT,
OR SELF-INTEGRATION, IS THE PURPOSE
OF ALL TRUE PSYCHOLOGY.

CONFLICT EXISTS ONLY TO INCREASE CONSCIOUSNESS.
C.G.Jung

THIS SELF LENDS ITSELF TO THAT SELF,
AND THAT SELF TO THIS SELF,
THEY COALESCE, OR ARE WEDDED TOGETHER.
WITH THIS ASPECT WE ARE UNITED WITH THIS WORLD
AND WITH THAT ASPECT UNITED WITH YONDER WORLD.
The Vedas

TWO BIRDS, FAST BOUND COMPANIONS,
CLASP CLOSE THE SELFSAME TREE OF LIFE.
The Upanishads

TO MAKE OF YOURSELF OF TWAIN
ONE NEW HUMAN BEING, SO MAKING PEACE.
The Bible

HEALING THROUGH PAST LIFE MEMORY

Dr Joel Whitton Ph.D.

Past lives affect us today. Many people are starting to experience deep personal transformation thanks to regression to past lives in which part of our consciousness was 'frozen' in trauma and regret.

◊

'In the healing of any traumatic neurosis, there's an element that demands repetition of the causative event to bring the trauma into the conscious mind. Making conscious, under hypnosis, a traumatic event which took place in a previous existence can lead to cessation of physical and psychological disorders.'

The following are extracts from the case study of a client of Dr Whitton who is given the fictitious name of Michael Gollander:-

"...he felt himself inside the knight's body, on horseback watching a woman with a baby in her arms begging to be spared. 'I am staring at her the way someone else might stare at a worm,' Michael later recounted. 'No sympathy, no compassion.' The act of lowering his lance and running it through the infant and into the mother brought him out of the trance with tears running down his cheeks. He knew he was responsible but wanted neither to accept nor believe what he had seen..."

"...something was happening; some kind of slow thaw seemed to be at work in the icebox of his psyche. It was encouraging but there was much more to experience in that lifetime and in other lives too..."

"...Michael understood why, in this life, he felt a compulsive need to punish himself..."

"...in another lifetime Michael shook convulsively on Dr Whitton's floor as he grappled, at uncomfortably close quarters, with another traumatic memory... Michael, who in this life is incapable of telling serious untruth, shuddered at the memories..."

"...yet there were encouraging signs that Michael was undergoing deep and positive changes. Although the guilt and sense of dread

maintained their obstinacy, he was more intuitive, more assertive and more at ease, both with himself and with others..."

"...after more than three years of probing Michael's reincarnational history, Dr Whitton sensed he was ready to sneak up on a life that should, with luck, be the catalyst that would release eight centuries of bottled-up emotion..."

"...the next few sessions would prove to be the most arduous of them all. Reassured by his visit to the interlife, Michael began to tackle - often hesitatingly and never willingly - traumatic episodes from the life of Julia M. .... time and time again, Michael's body arched and thrashed across Dr Whitton's floor as he confronted what he hadn't wanted to remember. Screaming, weeping, protesting and sighing, he..."

"...Michael felt the oppression of centuries drain from his body, leaving him with a hitherto unknown sensation of well-being. No longer was his relationship with his wife fraught with a sense of dread; his guilt and self-loathing ebbed away, and all absent-minded inclination to do away with himself evaporated. He discovered he could look into the mirror each morning without despairing and, when he fed the pigeons and gave money to the derelicts on the street, he found he was motivated by joy as well as by compassion."

"Friends and relatives detected changes in Michael's attitude towards life. He managed to shed a puritanical predisposition towards leisure and pleasure that enabled him to relax more easily and feel freer when, for example, he danced with his wife. Michael's wife could hardly believe his transformation. 'He's been freed from preoccupation,' she said. 'His mind is no longer his jailer.'"

"There were other dividends. In becoming aware of his personal tapestry of cause and effect spanning eight hundred years, Michael discovered that his concept of reality had been thoroughly overhauled. 'I have been allowed,' he said, speaking of his visits to the interlife, the place between lifetimes, 'the barest glimpse of levels of creation that are far above anything I can ever begin to put into words. I was made to feel that everything we do has meaning at the highest level. Our sufferings are not random; they are merely part of an eternal plan more complex and awe-inspiring than we are capable of imagining.'"

◊

AS WE FEEL THE EMOTIONS SUPPRESSED FOR SO LONG AROUND THE DIFFICULTY OF THE EARTH EXPERIENCE, WE FREE OURSELVES FOR AN UNDERSTANDING AND AN ALIGNMENT WHICH WILL TOTALLY TRANSFORM OUR LIVES.

EXPRESS EVERYTHING YOU FEEL AND DO NOT STOP EXPRESSING, EMOTIONALLY AND OTHERWISE, UNTIL YOU HAVE REALLY FINISHED.

GALACTIC ROUTE HOME

WE LOST TOUCH WITH OUR SOULS
FELL
SOULS AWAIT US
DARKEST NOW
BLACK VORTICES AROUND THE CENTRE
CHOOSE THE CENTRE
ACCEPT
RELAX - RELEASE - LET GO
AT THE BOTTOM
CENTRE POINT OF ENERGIES
SURROUNDED BY WHIRLWINDS
THIS IS THE HARDEST POINT
EXTREME SURROUNDS
CHOICE
WE FELL - LOST - FORGOT - SEPARATED
LONG TIME - ODYSSEY
WRONG PERCEPTIONS
FAULT IN MIND
MIND HAS NOT NOTICED THE FALL
IDENTITY SPINS OFF CENTRE IN TIME/SPACE
CHOICE NOW
I CHOOSE CENTRE
DIFFICULT NOW - STRONG ENERGIES
BRAIN WILL RELEASE
TENSION OLD HABIT
RELAXATION NEW HABIT
ALL DISSOLVES - SEEN FOR WHAT IT IS - & WHAT
REMAINS IS THAT GROUND LEVEL OF BEING
REUNION OF SOULS
DARKEST NOW - DAWN SOON - PEACE
YOU WILL SEE. I WILL SEE. I CHOOSE PEACE
I TRUST THE PROCESS. I MOVE CORRECTLY
I RELEASE THE PAST. I NEW AM
ALL MY BEINGS EVERYWHERE WITHIN TIME/SPACE
I ACCEPT AND I AM WHOLE.

THE STORY OF AN EMOTIONALLY LOST CHILD

'DIBS' by Virginia Axline

He would not talk. He would not play. Judged mentally defective, he was oblivious both to other children and to his teacher; in reality he was a brilliant, lonely child trapped in a prison of fear and rage, a prison from which only he could release himself. And through psychotherapy and love, he did.

'...Dibs had lived in two worlds for too long a time for any of us to expect immediate and complete integration. Dibs' social progress was the most important factor in his development now. There was no question about his ability - unless one wanted to raise the question of wasted ability. But at this stage personal and social adjustment was more important than a display of his ability.'

'...He was achieving new horizons for himself socially and emotionally. His intellectual ability had become a barrier and a refuge from a world he feared. It had been defensive, self protective behaviour. It had been his isolation.'

'...As Dibs stood before me now his head was up. He had a feeling of security deep inside himself. He was building a sense of responsibility for his feelings. His feelings of hate and revenge had been tempered with mercy.'

'...Dibs was building a concept of self as he groped through the tangled brambles of his mixed-up feelings. He could hate and he could love. He could condemn and he could pardon. He was learning through experience that feelings can twist and turn and lose their sharp edges. He was learning responsible control as well as expression of his feelings.'

'...Through this increasing self-knowledge he would be free to use his capacities and emotions more constructively.'

◊ *DIBS* ◊

WHEN THE WINDS CEASE YOU SHALL BE HOME

"I am here. All will clear with time. All the turbulence, confusion, pain and conflict will go and all that will remain will be clarity and peace. You are who I am. We are the universal one of all things and all beings. I am the peace beyond all understanding. As you attune to your centre, to me, you feel the truth of this.

"The winds will stop. Nothing is wasted. You grow. We approach. The winds will cease. Give your emotions the time they need. The lostness you feel is the noise of the winds. The winds will cease for there is only one true reality from which no being, no thing, will be lost. Give yourself the time. Give yourself the time. You cannot be lost.

"Hold to your purpose. Trust the parts of your life to dance and weave an awakening directing you to the centre of yourself. Creation awaits you. Creation, your creation, moves to arouse you to your true reality. It is a dance. It is a movement. You shall return. You are returning. There is only one reality. Know this and know you are safe.

"When the winds cease you shall be home. Hear the cosmic OM. Feel the gold and sunlit oneness of the egg and sphere of creation. The peace you seek you will find. Give your feelings and emotions the time they need and you shall return home complete. Then the magical paradox of feeling you never left home will dawn within and about you."

Sananda - The Universal One

THE BIRTH OF THE DIVINE EARTH CHILD

Barbara Hand Clow

The sky teaching for Earth has finished. The people of Earth are ready to know divinity in their hearts by individually facing their unconsciousness and inner darkness. We are all asked to become courageous.

Here is the big secret: we can't have knowledge in a multi-dimensional way unless it can be felt. That is why there has been so much suffering on Earth which will continue until feelings evolve. The silver cord into the solar plexus connects the astral body to the physical body and the solar plexus must be cleared of pain in order to free the astral body and awaken the stellar body.

If the lessons from Sirius are going to be available on Earth, we must become conscious about our evolution by learning to clear the emotional body. Skills for doing so exist in the memory banks of all individuals. When the emotional body is cleared the brain is capable of multi-dimensional access and lessons from Sirius will be available on Earth.

In the late 20th century each individual will be personally called to overcome his or her own sense of separation. At this time the ego will become dysfunctional and will evolve into a higher form. Dimensional shifts are a requirement for ascension. The ancient Egyptians knew how to accelerate their bodies to be multi-dimensional. We have to clear our emotional bodies.

◊

When I had realised I could decide to change reality, getting myself to do anything was like trying to crawl out of a deep sleep, because we learn to *FEEL* in the third dimension. →

In this life, as I have tried to act with consciousness, all the pain and resistance I had experienced in violent past lives resurfaced and engulfed me. Each time I have awakened a new aspect of myself, I have had to go back through the maze of pain and resistance at the cellular level in order to open new spaces within myself. I have to let go of every single belief system in which I was limited in any way in my search for the pathway to the centre of creation.

The daykeeper awaits the return which will bring the opening of the new dawn. The daykeeper will wait for the people who wear no mask, who open their hearts and trust life on Earth enough to look into the deepest parts of the self. Seeing such raw truth is a great purification.

We must see that each time we came to Earth and then left without finding our souls we created a place in ourselves that denies the spirit now. To regenerate ourselves we must integrate every action we have ever done and then create spirit right in that place we once denied.

◊

A healing crisis will occur for us all when the stellar link is established (judging by crop patterns found in England, this happened in 1990) for then all the experiences of pain and fear residing within ourselves from our own EVOLUTION will need to be cleared. This is leading us into our place of deepest sadness, a place in our hearts where the painful experiences exist right next to a place of waiting for peace inside.

There is a feeling that tells us to open up the locus of inner suffering, fear and despair. Then, through time, energy and peace will be able to radiate from the heart again.

KEY STATEMENTS ON EMOTIONAL HEALING

I We now need to allow ourselves more emotions of all types than we had previously felt existed or were possible. We need to feel the chaos of emotions held suppressed in lost consciousness. These chaotic emotions have been seen as the problem of creation instead of the saviour they are going to turn out to be.

II When we have cleared enough of our surface confusion we are going to need to reclaim the rest of us. This is the part of us that has not expressed itself yet in this present life because this denied part had to wait until it could be accepted before it could come forward for clearance.

III In healing our emotions we must allow them to tell us how upset they have become. The understanding needed is: in hearing from our emotions unconditionally, we have taken the step of accepting them wherever they are. We must accept our feelings in order to evolve them. We cannot beat feelings into the appropriate shape. Feelings have to be accepted as they are and then evolved.

IV Everything has to be seen and accepted for what it really is to be truly understood. Knowing what something really is is necessary in order to deal with it in the right way. What was lost returns when we forgive ourselves for denying it and accept it. This does not mean forgiving ourselves for the behaviour. It means accepting the behaviour and forgiving ourselves for not having accepted it before as part of us and our living experience.

V As we feel the emotions suppressed for so long around the difficulty of the Earth experience, we free ourselves for an understanding and an alignment which will totally transform our lives. We need to express everything we really feel and we should not stop expressing, emotionally and otherwise, until we have really finished.

VI Spiritual teaching should not be directing us to lift above and drop off the physical and emotional bodies and try to return to essence in the Godhead without them. This has been a massive spiritual misunderstanding on Earth. The reality is that this approach will not work because what is ours is ours, and we cannot drop it off. The way is to evolve, and to evolve we must accept it.

VII We have always suppressed the feeling that God was not there for us in the way God was there for others. We have never felt the acceptance we have wanted for ourselves in creation. We need to feel the shock and confusion we hold for never being able to live the way we have always wanted to live. We need to feel the deep sadness underneath the shock for the helplessness we have experienced in trying to change our situation.

VIII When we reach our deepest emotions, we may for a while find ourselves unable to move as though everything we have realised so far makes no difference at all. This is a time for us to keep going. It is a time to keep feeling, to keep allowing time and space and consciousness for whatever we are experiencing. We need to carry on without interference from people who do not understand.

IX The more we have limited the expression of some emotions, the more the capacity to experience and express all the other emotions is also affected.

X The most important thing is for us to become as real as possible with ourselves and others by allowing as much of our true feelings as possible to express each day.

XI Until we break through the pattern of self-judgment and self-criticism, until we feel ourselves staying open to emotions without passing sentence, we will continue to undermine our efforts and defeat all our good intentions toward feeling whole.

XIII We need to recognise every feeling and thought we would otherwise push away or ignore. Any feeling can evolve into another feeling of greater understanding if it is felt and expressed and not pressured but given time and space. ◊

KEY SHORT STATEMENTS ON EMOTIONAL HEALING

I Feeling is healing. Stay open to feelings.

II Conflict exists only to increase consciousness.

III The stronger the resistance, the closer we are coming to the truth.

IV Different parts of us have different feelings. We need to validate all of them.

V Nearly everyone has believed in the futility of emotional expression.

VI The place of true feelings is filled in by confusion. In this confusion we often experience false feelings we are convinced we have.

VII Freeing ourselves of how we are 'meant' to be allows our true sensitivity and true reality to return.

VIII The way to create change in our lives is for us to be as real as we can with ALL our feelings.

IX Error decisions, from past experience, limit our awareness and inhibit our creative response to the present moment.

X Societal conditioning has taught everyone to talk in generalisations and to control emotions and thus lock up the free flow of experience.

XI A good way to awaken spirit in matter is to admit how it feels to BE spirit in matter.

XII Deeply suppressed emotions are not aware that they are going to heal. ◊

SIRIAN TEACHING III FOR PLANET EARTH

HUMANITY HAS EXPERIENCED CONSCIOUSNESS AND UNCONSCIOUSNESS

YOU HAVE FREE-WILL TO CHOOSE

YOU HAVE THE ABILITY TO BE ON EARTH AND IN OTHER DIMENSIONS SIMULTANEOUSLY

TO TOTALLY REGAIN YOUR TRUE IDENTITY AS ONENESS-WITH-ALL-THINGS YOU MUST AWAKEN WHILE ON EARTH AND IN A PHYSICAL BODY

SPIRIT/INTELLECT/THINKING WILL NO LONGER BE SEPARATE FROM THE SOURCE/GOD WHEN IT IS EQUAL WITH WILL/MATTER/HUMAN

YOU WILL ASSIST WITH THE BIRTH OF THE CHILD OF THE CREATOR ON EARTH

PREPARE NOW FOR THE BIRTH OF THE DIVINE EARTH CHILD - THE CALIBRATION OF STELLAR DIMENSIONS INTO THIRD DIMENSIONAL FORM

THE FOLLOWING BOOKS ARE RECOMMENDED & ARE AVAILABLE FROM THE ACORN CENTRE:

ACORN BOOK OF BIRTHING THE COSMIC CHILD [£4] This book follows on from 'Acorn Emotional Healing'. Quote: 'Surely it is now the time for the new child to come forth from the shadows of my inner world into the light of the Earthly world in order to fulfil the destiny which is encoded within the mystery of the deepest centre of the truth of my being'.

HEART OF THE CHRISTOS - STARSEEDING FROM THE PLEIADES by Barbara Hand Clow [£7] The return to Earth of the Star people... remembering all past lives... Sirian teaching III for planet Earth... the importance of Avebury Stone Circle in England... emotional balancing... birthing the child of the creator on Earth... Quote: 'You have the ability to be on Earth and in other dimensions simultaneously'.

THE LEGEND OF ALTAZAR - A FRAGMENT OF THE TRUE HISTORY OF PLANET EARTH by Solara [£8] A group of souls share experiences down through time from Lemuria, An, Atlantis, Egypt and on to the present day. Quote: 'The time has come to make an end to our denials. Can you finally step forward into the light of self forgiveness? Only then shall you experience true healing and completion'.

RIGHT USE OF WILL - HEALING & EVOLVING THE EMOTIONAL BODY by Ceanne DeRohan [£6] Many of the universal concepts of deep psychological understanding in 'Acorn Emotional Healing' are from this book. The story of humanity evolving through Pan, Lemuria, Atlantis and on to today's challenge: evolution to a new level of consciousness.

DIBS - IN SEARCH OF SELF by Virginia Axline [£6] The moving story of an emotionally lost child who found his own way back. Quote: 'He would not talk. He would not play. Judged mentally defective, he was oblivious both to other children and to his teacher; in reality he was a brilliant, lonely child trapped in a prison of fear & rage, a prison from which only he could free himself. And through understanding and love he did'.

LIVING BEYOND FEAR by Jeanne Segal Ph.D. [£4] A workbook for unblocking the powerful emotions that prevent healing. Quote: 'The passage from fear to wisdom and hope is one that requires us to connect with feelings that we may dislike or disapprove of. However, this experience not only frees us from patterns that limit health but transforms our lives in ways that strengthen us physically, emotionally and spiritually'.

POST & PACKING

P&P UK: first book: £1; additional books: +50p each. P&P Overseas: surface or airmail charges can be invoiced to you at cost. For full booklist phone, visit or write to: The ACORN Centre, Spindlewood, Watery Lane, Lower Westholme, Pilton, Shepton Mallet, Somerset, BA4 4EL, UK. Further copies of 'ACORN EMOTIONAL HEALING' are £4 each plus p&p.

☆ ☆ ☆ Telephone: 074 989 338 ☆ ☆ ☆

CONFLICT EXISTS
ONLY TO INCREASE
CONSCIOUSNESS

C.G.JUNG